TABLE OF CONTENTS

TABLE OF CONTENTS (continued)

TABLE OF CONTENTS (continued)

TABLE OF CONTENTS (continued)

USEFUL INFORMATION

α – The percentage of a given hop that is alpha acid. A hop with a higher alpha acid percentage will contribute more bitterness to the beer

Wort – unfermented beer

Original Gravity (OG) – the specific gravity of the wort, generally measured with a hydrometer just prior to the addition of yeast

Final Gravity (FG) – the specific gravity of the fermented beer

ABV – Alcohol By Volume. This can be estimated using the following formula:

$$ABV = (OG - FG) * 131$$

Beer Color – A gradient of the description of beer colors is shown below

	Black
	Brown
	Amber
	Copper
	Golden
	Pale

BEER NAME

Beer Style: _____   Date Brewed: _____

Batch Number: _____   Batch Size: _____

Specialty Grains

GRAIN TYPE	AMOUNT

Fermentables

FERMENTABLE TYPE	AMOUNT

Hops

HOP TYPE	AMOUNT	α	ADDITION TIME

Yeast Type:

Grain Steeping Time: _____   Boil Time: _____

Cooling Method: _____

Original Gravity: _____ Final Gravity: _____ ABV: _____

Brewing Notes:

_____

_____

_____

_____

_____

_____

Fermentation:_____

_____

_____

_____

Notes on Finished Beer

Color: _____

Taste: _____

_____

_____

Other: _____

_____

_____

_____

BEER NAME

Beer Style: _____   Date Brewed: _____

Batch Number: _____   Batch Size: _____

Specialty Grains

GRAIN TYPE	AMOUNT

Fermentables

FERMENTABLE TYPE	AMOUNT

Hops

HOP TYPE	AMOUNT	α	ADDITION TIME

Yeast Type:

_____

_____

Grain Steeping Time: _____ Boil Time: _____

Cooling Method: _____

Original Gravity: _____ Final Gravity: _____ ABV: _____

Brewing Notes:

_____
_____
_____
_____
_____
_____
_____

Fermentation:_____

_____
_____
_____

Notes on Finished Beer

Color: _____

Taste: _____

_____
_____

Other: _____

_____
_____
_____

BEER NAME

Beer Style: _____   Date Brewed: _____

Batch Number: _____   Batch Size: _____

Specialty Grains

GRAIN TYPE	AMOUNT

Fermentables

FERMENTABLE TYPE	AMOUNT

Hops

HOP TYPE	AMOUNT	α	ADDITION TIME

Yeast Type:

_____

_____

Grain Steeping Time: _____   Boil Time: _____

Cooling Method: _____

Original Gravity: _____ Final Gravity: _____ ABV: _____

Brewing Notes:

_____

_____

_____

_____

_____

_____

_____

Fermentation: _____

_____

_____

_____

Notes on Finished Beer

Color: _____

Taste: _____

_____

_____

Other: _____

_____

_____

_____

BEER NAME

Beer Style: _____   Date Brewed: _____

Batch Number: _____   Batch Size: _____

Specialty Grains

GRAIN TYPE	AMOUNT

Fermentables

FERMENTABLE TYPE	AMOUNT

Hops

HOP TYPE	AMOUNT	α	ADDITION TIME

Yeast Type:

_____

_____

Grain Steeping Time: _____   Boil Time: _____

Cooling Method: _____

Original Gravity: _____ Final Gravity: _____ ABV: _____

Brewing Notes:

_____

_____

_____

_____

_____

_____

_____

Fermentation: _____

_____

_____

_____

_____

Notes on Finished Beer

Color: _____

Taste: _____

_____

_____

Other: _____

_____

_____

_____

BEER NAME

Beer Style: _____   Date Brewed: _____

Batch Number: _____   Batch Size: _____

Specialty Grains

GRAIN TYPE	AMOUNT

Fermentables

FERMENTABLE TYPE	AMOUNT

Hops

HOP TYPE	AMOUNT	α	ADDITION TIME

Yeast Type:

_____

_____

Grain Steeping Time: _____ Boil Time: _____

Cooling Method: _____

Original Gravity: _____ Final Gravity: _____ ABV: _____

Brewing Notes:

_____

_____

_____

_____

_____

_____

_____

Fermentation:_____

_____

_____

_____

Notes on Finished Beer

Color: _____

Taste: _____

_____

_____

Other: _____

_____

_____

BEER NAME

Beer Style: _____   Date Brewed: _____

Batch Number: _____   Batch Size: _____

Specialty Grains

GRAIN TYPE	AMOUNT

Fermentables

FERMENTABLE TYPE	AMOUNT

Hops

HOP TYPE	AMOUNT	α	ADDITION TIME

Yeast Type:

Grain Steeping Time: _____   Boil Time: _____

Cooling Method: _____

Original Gravity: _____ Final Gravity: _____ ABV: _____

Brewing Notes:

_____

_____

_____

_____

_____

_____

_____

Fermentation:_____

_____

_____

_____

_____

Notes on Finished Beer

Color: _____

Taste: _____

_____

_____

Other: _____

_____

_____

_____

BEER NAME

Beer Style: _____ Date Brewed: _____

Batch Number: _____ Batch Size: _____

Specialty Grains

GRAIN TYPE	AMOUNT

Fermentables

FERMENTABLE TYPE	AMOUNT

Hops

HOP TYPE	AMOUNT	α	ADDITION TIME

Yeast Type:

_____

_____

Grain Steeping Time: _____   Boil Time: _____

Cooling Method: _____

Original Gravity: _____ Final Gravity: _____ ABV: _____

Brewing Notes:

_____
_____
_____
_____
_____
_____
_____

Fermentation:_____

_____
_____
_____
_____

Notes on Finished Beer

Color: _____

Taste: _____

_____
_____

Other: _____

_____
_____
_____

BEER NAME

Beer Style: _____   Date Brewed: _____

Batch Number: _____   Batch Size: _____

Specialty Grains

GRAIN TYPE	AMOUNT

Fermentables

FERMENTABLE TYPE	AMOUNT

Hops

HOP TYPE	AMOUNT	α	ADDITION TIME

Yeast Type:

_____

_____

Grain Steeping Time: _____ Boil Time: _____

Cooling Method: _____

Original Gravity: _____ Final Gravity: _____ ABV: _____

Brewing Notes:

_____

_____

_____

_____

_____

_____

_____

Fermentation:_____

_____

_____

_____

_____

Notes on Finished Beer

Color: _____

Taste: _____

_____

_____

Other: _____

_____

_____

_____

BEER NAME

Beer Style: _____   Date Brewed: _____

Batch Number: _____   Batch Size: _____

Specialty Grains

GRAIN TYPE	AMOUNT

Fermentables

FERMENTABLE TYPE	AMOUNT

Hops

HOP TYPE	AMOUNT	α	ADDITION TIME

Yeast Type:

Grain Steeping Time: _____   Boil Time: _____

Cooling Method: _____

Original Gravity: _____ Final Gravity: _____ ABV: _____

Brewing Notes:

_____

_____

_____

_____

_____

_____

_____

Fermentation:_____

_____

_____

_____

_____

Notes on Finished Beer

Color: _____

Taste: _____

_____

_____

Other: _____

_____

_____

_____

BEER NAME

Beer Style: _____ Date Brewed: _____

Batch Number: _____ Batch Size: _____

Specialty Grains

GRAIN TYPE	AMOUNT

Fermentables

FERMENTABLE TYPE	AMOUNT

Hops

HOP TYPE	AMOUNT	α	ADDITION TIME

Yeast Type:

_____

_____

Grain Steeping Time: _____   Boil Time: _____

Cooling Method: _____

Original Gravity: _____ Final Gravity: _____ ABV: _____

Brewing Notes:

_____

_____

_____

_____

_____

_____

_____

Fermentation:_____

_____

_____

_____

Notes on Finished Beer

Color: _____

Taste: _____

_____

_____

Other: _____

_____

_____

_____

BEER NAME

Beer Style: _____   Date Brewed: _____

Batch Number: _____   Batch Size: _____

Specialty Grains

GRAIN TYPE	AMOUNT

Fermentables

FERMENTABLE TYPE	AMOUNT

Hops

HOP TYPE	AMOUNT	α	ADDITION TIME

Yeast Type:

_____

_____

Grain Steeping Time: _____   Boil Time: _____

Cooling Method: _____

Original Gravity: _____ Final Gravity: _____ ABV: _____

Brewing Notes:

_____
_____
_____
_____
_____
_____
_____

Fermentation:_____
_____
_____
_____

Notes on Finished Beer

Color: _____

Taste: _____
_____
_____

Other: _____
_____
_____

BEER NAME

Beer Style: _____   Date Brewed: _____

Batch Number: _____   Batch Size: _____

Specialty Grains

GRAIN TYPE	AMOUNT

Fermentables

FERMENTABLE TYPE	AMOUNT

Hops

HOP TYPE	AMOUNT	α	ADDITION TIME

Yeast Type:

_____

_____

Grain Steeping Time: _____   Boil Time: _____

Cooling Method: _____

Original Gravity: _____ Final Gravity: _____ ABV: _____

Brewing Notes:

_____

_____

_____

_____

_____

_____

_____

Fermentation: _____

_____

_____

_____

Notes on Finished Beer

Color: _____

Taste: _____

_____

_____

Other: _____

_____

_____

_____

BEER NAME

Beer Style: _____   Date Brewed: _____

Batch Number: _____   Batch Size: _____

Specialty Grains

GRAIN TYPE	AMOUNT

Fermentables

FERMENTABLE TYPE	AMOUNT

Hops

HOP TYPE	AMOUNT	α	ADDITION TIME

Yeast Type:

_____

_____

Grain Steeping Time: _____   Boil Time: _____

Cooling Method: _____

Original Gravity: _____ Final Gravity: _____ ABV: _____

Brewing Notes:

_____

_____

_____

_____

_____

_____

_____

Fermentation:_____

_____

_____

_____

_____

Notes on Finished Beer

Color: _____

Taste: _____

_____

_____

Other: _____

_____

_____

_____

BEER NAME

Beer Style: _____   Date Brewed: _____

Batch Number: _____   Batch Size: _____

Specialty Grains

GRAIN TYPE	AMOUNT

Fermentables

FERMENTABLE TYPE	AMOUNT

Hops

HOP TYPE	AMOUNT	α	ADDITION TIME

Yeast Type:

_____

_____

Grain Steeping Time: _____   Boil Time: _____

Cooling Method: _____

Original Gravity: _____ Final Gravity: _____ ABV: _____

Brewing Notes:

_____

_____

_____

_____

_____

_____

_____

Fermentation:_____

_____

_____

_____

Notes on Finished Beer

Color: _____

Taste: _____

_____

_____

Other: _____

_____

_____

_____

BEER NAME

Beer Style: _____   Date Brewed: _____

Batch Number: _____   Batch Size: _____

Specialty Grains

GRAIN TYPE	AMOUNT

Fermentables

FERMENTABLE TYPE	AMOUNT

Hops

HOP TYPE	AMOUNT	α	ADDITION TIME

Yeast Type:

_____

_____

Grain Steeping Time: _____   Boil Time: _____

Cooling Method: _____

Original Gravity: _____ Final Gravity: _____ ABV: _____

Brewing Notes:

_____

_____

_____

_____

_____

_____

_____

Fermentation:_____

_____

_____

_____

_____

Notes on Finished Beer

Color: _____

Taste: _____

_____

_____

Other: _____

_____

_____

_____

BEER NAME

Beer Style: _____   Date Brewed: _____

Batch Number: _____   Batch Size: _____

Specialty Grains

GRAIN TYPE	AMOUNT

Fermentables

FERMENTABLE TYPE	AMOUNT

Hops

HOP TYPE	AMOUNT	α	ADDITION TIME

Yeast Type:

_____

_____

Grain Steeping Time: _____   Boil Time: _____

Cooling Method: _____

Original Gravity: _____ Final Gravity: _____ ABV: _____

Brewing Notes:

_____

_____

_____

_____

_____

_____

_____

Fermentation:_____

_____

_____

_____

_____

Notes on Finished Beer

Color: _____

Taste: _____

_____

_____

Other: _____

_____

_____

_____

BEER NAME

Beer Style: _____   Date Brewed: _____

Batch Number: _____   Batch Size: _____

Specialty Grains

GRAIN TYPE	AMOUNT

Fermentables

FERMENTABLE TYPE	AMOUNT

Hops

HOP TYPE	AMOUNT	α	ADDITION TIME

Yeast Type:

_____

Grain Steeping Time: _____   Boil Time: _____

Cooling Method: _____

Original Gravity: _____ Final Gravity: _____ ABV: _____

Brewing Notes:

_____

_____

_____

_____

_____

_____

_____

Fermentation:_____

_____

_____

_____

Notes on Finished Beer

Color: _____

Taste: _____

_____

_____

Other: _____

_____

_____

BEER NAME

Beer Style: _____   Date Brewed: _____

Batch Number: _____   Batch Size: _____

Specialty Grains

GRAIN TYPE	AMOUNT

Fermentables

FERMENTABLE TYPE	AMOUNT

Hops

HOP TYPE	AMOUNT	α	ADDITION TIME

Yeast Type:

Grain Steeping Time: _____   Boil Time: _____

Cooling Method: _____

Original Gravity: _____ Final Gravity: _____ ABV: _____

Brewing Notes:

_____

_____

_____

_____

_____

_____

_____

Fermentation:_____

_____

_____

_____

Notes on Finished Beer

Color: _____

Taste: _____

_____

_____

Other: _____

_____

_____

BEER NAME

_____

Beer Style: _____ Date Brewed: _____

Batch Number: _____ Batch Size: _____

Specialty Grains

GRAIN TYPE	AMOUNT

Fermentables

FERMENTABLE TYPE	AMOUNT

Hops

HOP TYPE	AMOUNT	α	ADDITION TIME

Yeast Type:

_____

_____

Grain Steeping Time: _____   Boil Time: _____

Cooling Method: _____

Original Gravity: _____ Final Gravity: _____ ABV: _____

Brewing Notes:

_____

_____

_____

_____

_____

_____

_____

Fermentation:_____

_____

_____

_____

_____

Notes on Finished Beer

Color: _____

Taste: _____

_____

_____

Other: _____

_____

_____

_____

Beer Style: _____   Date Brewed: _____

Batch Number: _____   Batch Size: _____

Specialty Grains

GRAIN TYPE	AMOUNT

Fermentables

FERMENTABLE TYPE	AMOUNT

Hops

HOP TYPE	AMOUNT	α	ADDITION TIME

Yeast Type:

_____

_____

Grain Steeping Time: _____ Boil Time: _____

Cooling Method: _____

Original Gravity: _____ Final Gravity: _____ ABV: _____

Brewing Notes:

_____

_____

_____

_____

_____

_____

_____

Fermentation:_____

_____

_____

_____

Notes on Finished Beer

Color: _____

Taste: _____

_____

_____

Other: _____

_____

_____

_____

BEER NAME

Beer Style: _____   Date Brewed: _____

Batch Number: _____   Batch Size: _____

Specialty Grains

GRAIN TYPE	AMOUNT

Fermentables

FERMENTABLE TYPE	AMOUNT

Hops

HOP TYPE	AMOUNT	α	ADDITION TIME

Yeast Type:

Grain Steeping Time: _____ Boil Time: _____

Cooling Method: _____

Original Gravity: _____ Final Gravity: _____ ABV: _____

Brewing Notes:

_____

_____

_____

_____

_____

_____

_____

Fermentation:_____

_____

_____

_____

_____

Notes on Finished Beer

Color: _____

Taste: _____

_____

_____

Other: _____

_____

_____

_____

Beer Style: _____   Date Brewed: _____

Batch Number: _____   Batch Size: _____

Specialty Grains

GRAIN TYPE	AMOUNT

Fermentables

FERMENTABLE TYPE	AMOUNT

Hops

HOP TYPE	AMOUNT	α	ADDITION TIME

Yeast Type:

_____

_____

Grain Steeping Time: _____   Boil Time: _____

Cooling Method: _____

Original Gravity: _____ Final Gravity: _____ ABV: _____

Brewing Notes:

_____

_____

_____

_____

_____

_____

Fermentation:_____

_____

_____

_____

_____

Notes on Finished Beer

Color: _____

Taste: _____

_____

_____

Other: _____

_____

_____

BEER NAME

Beer Style: _____   Date Brewed: _____

Batch Number: _____   Batch Size: _____

Specialty Grains

GRAIN TYPE	AMOUNT

Fermentables

FERMENTABLE TYPE	AMOUNT

Hops

HOP TYPE	AMOUNT	α	ADDITION TIME

Yeast Type:

_____

_____

Grain Steeping Time: _____   Boil Time: _____

Cooling Method: _____

Original Gravity: _____ Final Gravity: _____ ABV: _____

Brewing Notes:

_____

_____

_____

_____

_____

_____

_____

Fermentation:_____

_____

_____

_____

_____

Notes on Finished Beer

Color: _____

Taste: _____

_____

_____

Other: _____

_____

_____

Beer Style: _____   Date Brewed: _____

Batch Number: _____   Batch Size: _____

Specialty Grains

GRAIN TYPE	AMOUNT

Fermentables

FERMENTABLE TYPE	AMOUNT

Hops

HOP TYPE	AMOUNT	α	ADDITION TIME

Yeast Type:

_____

_____

Grain Steeping Time: _____ Boil Time: _____

Cooling Method: _____

Original Gravity: _____ Final Gravity: _____ ABV: _____

Brewing Notes:

_____

_____

_____

_____

_____

_____

_____

Fermentation:_____

_____

_____

_____

_____

Notes on Finished Beer

Color: _____

Taste: _____

_____

_____

Other: _____

_____

_____

_____

BEER NAME

Beer Style: _____   Date Brewed: _____

Batch Number: _____   Batch Size: _____

Specialty Grains

GRAIN TYPE	AMOUNT

Fermentables

FERMENTABLE TYPE	AMOUNT

Hops

HOP TYPE	AMOUNT	α	ADDITION TIME

Yeast Type:

Grain Steeping Time: _____   Boil Time: _____

Cooling Method: _____

Original Gravity: _____ Final Gravity: _____ ABV: _____

Brewing Notes:

_____

_____

_____

_____

_____

_____

_____

Fermentation:_____

_____

_____

_____

_____

Notes on Finished Beer

Color: _____

Taste: _____

_____

_____

_____

Other: _____

_____

_____

_____

BEER NAME

Beer Style: _____   Date Brewed: _____

Batch Number: _____   Batch Size: _____

Specialty Grains

GRAIN TYPE	AMOUNT

Fermentables

FERMENTABLE TYPE	AMOUNT

Hops

HOP TYPE	AMOUNT	α	ADDITION TIME

Yeast Type:

_____

_____

Grain Steeping Time: _____   Boil Time: _____

Cooling Method: _____

Original Gravity: _____ Final Gravity: _____ ABV: _____

Brewing Notes:

_____

_____

_____

_____

_____

_____

_____

Fermentation:_____

_____

_____

_____

_____

Notes on Finished Beer

Color: _____

Taste: _____

_____

_____

Other: _____

_____

_____

_____

BEER NAME

Beer Style: _____   Date Brewed: _____

Batch Number: _____   Batch Size: _____

Specialty Grains

GRAIN TYPE	AMOUNT

Fermentables

FERMENTABLE TYPE	AMOUNT

Hops

HOP TYPE	AMOUNT	α	ADDITION TIME

Yeast Type:

Grain Steeping Time: _____   Boil Time: _____

Cooling Method: _____

Original Gravity: _____ Final Gravity: _____ ABV: _____

Brewing Notes:

_____
_____
_____
_____
_____
_____
_____

Fermentation:_____

_____
_____
_____
_____

Notes on Finished Beer

Color: _____

Taste: _____

_____
_____

Other: _____

_____
_____
_____

Beer Style: _____   Date Brewed: _____

Batch Number: _____   Batch Size: _____

Specialty Grains

GRAIN TYPE	AMOUNT

Fermentables

FERMENTABLE TYPE	AMOUNT

Hops

HOP TYPE	AMOUNT	α	ADDITION TIME

Yeast Type:

_____

_____

Grain Steeping Time: _____   Boil Time: _____

Cooling Method: _____

Original Gravity: _____ Final Gravity: _____ ABV: _____

Brewing Notes:

_____

_____

_____

_____

_____

_____

_____

Fermentation:_____

_____

_____

_____

Notes on Finished Beer

Color: _____

Taste: _____

_____

_____

Other: _____

_____

_____

_____

Beer Style: _____   Date Brewed: _____

Batch Number: _____   Batch Size: _____

Specialty Grains

GRAIN TYPE	AMOUNT

Fermentables

FERMENTABLE TYPE	AMOUNT

Hops

HOP TYPE	AMOUNT	α	ADDITION TIME

Yeast Type:

Grain Steeping Time: _____   Boil Time: _____

Cooling Method: _____

Original Gravity: _____ Final Gravity: _____ ABV: _____

Brewing Notes:

_____

_____

_____

_____

_____

_____

_____

Fermentation:_____

_____

_____

_____

_____

Notes on Finished Beer

Color: _____

Taste: _____

_____

_____

Other: _____

_____

_____

_____

BEER NAME

Beer Style: _____   Date Brewed: _____

Batch Number: _____   Batch Size: _____

Specialty Grains

GRAIN TYPE	AMOUNT

Fermentables

FERMENTABLE TYPE	AMOUNT

Hops

HOP TYPE	AMOUNT	α	ADDITION TIME

Yeast Type:

Grain Steeping Time: _____   Boil Time: _____

Cooling Method: _____

Original Gravity: _____ Final Gravity: _____ ABV: _____

Brewing Notes:

_____

_____

_____

_____

_____

_____

_____

Fermentation:_____

_____

_____

_____

Notes on Finished Beer

Color: _____

Taste: _____

_____

_____

Other: _____

_____

_____

BEER NAME

Beer Style: _____   Date Brewed: _____

Batch Number: _____   Batch Size: _____

Specialty Grains

GRAIN TYPE	AMOUNT

Fermentables

FERMENTABLE TYPE	AMOUNT

Hops

HOP TYPE	AMOUNT	α	ADDITION TIME

Yeast Type:

_____

_____

Grain Steeping Time: _____   Boil Time: _____

Cooling Method: _____

Original Gravity: _____ Final Gravity: _____ ABV: _____

Brewing Notes:

_____

_____

_____

_____

_____

_____

_____

Fermentation:_____

_____

_____

_____

_____

Notes on Finished Beer

Color: _____

Taste: _____

_____

_____

Other: _____

_____

_____

_____

BEER NAME

Beer Style: _____   Date Brewed: _____

Batch Number: _____   Batch Size: _____

Specialty Grains

GRAIN TYPE	AMOUNT

Fermentables

FERMENTABLE TYPE	AMOUNT

Hops

HOP TYPE	AMOUNT	α	ADDITION TIME

Yeast Type:

Grain Steeping Time: _____   Boil Time: _____

Cooling Method: _____

Original Gravity: _____ Final Gravity: _____ ABV: _____

Brewing Notes:

_____

_____

_____

_____

_____

_____

_____

Fermentation:_____

_____

_____

_____

_____

Notes on Finished Beer

Color: _____

Taste: _____

_____

_____

Other: _____

_____

_____

_____

BEER NAME

Beer Style: _____   Date Brewed: _____

Batch Number: _____   Batch Size: _____

Specialty Grains

GRAIN TYPE	AMOUNT

Fermentables

FERMENTABLE TYPE	AMOUNT

Hops

HOP TYPE	AMOUNT	α	ADDITION TIME

Yeast Type:

_____

_____

Grain Steeping Time: _____   Boil Time: _____

Cooling Method: _____

Original Gravity: _____ Final Gravity: _____ ABV: _____

Brewing Notes:

_____
_____
_____
_____
_____
_____
_____

Fermentation:_____

_____
_____
_____
_____

Notes on Finished Beer

Color: _____

Taste: _____

_____
_____

Other: _____

_____
_____
_____

BEER NAME

Beer Style: _____   Date Brewed: _____

Batch Number: _____   Batch Size: _____

Specialty Grains

GRAIN TYPE	AMOUNT

Fermentables

FERMENTABLE TYPE	AMOUNT

Hops

HOP TYPE	AMOUNT	α	ADDITION TIME

Yeast Type:

_____

_____

Grain Steeping Time: _____   Boil Time: _____

Cooling Method: _____

Original Gravity: _____ Final Gravity: _____ ABV: _____

Brewing Notes:

_____

_____

_____

_____

_____

_____

_____

Fermentation:_____

_____

_____

_____

Notes on Finished Beer

Color: _____

Taste: _____

_____

_____

Other: _____

_____

_____

_____

BEER NAME

Beer Style: _____   Date Brewed: _____

Batch Number: _____   Batch Size: _____

Specialty Grains

GRAIN TYPE	AMOUNT

Fermentables

FERMENTABLE TYPE	AMOUNT

Hops

HOP TYPE	AMOUNT	α	ADDITION TIME

Yeast Type:

Grain Steeping Time: _____   Boil Time: _____

Cooling Method: _____

Original Gravity: _____ Final Gravity: _____ ABV: _____

Brewing Notes:

_____

_____

_____

_____

_____

_____

_____

Fermentation:_____

_____

_____

_____

_____

Notes on Finished Beer

Color: _____

Taste: _____

_____

_____

Other: _____

_____

_____

_____

BEER NAME

Beer Style: _____   Date Brewed: _____

Batch Number: _____   Batch Size: _____

Specialty Grains

GRAIN TYPE	AMOUNT

Fermentables

FERMENTABLE TYPE	AMOUNT

Hops

HOP TYPE	AMOUNT	α	ADDITION TIME

Yeast Type:

Grain Steeping Time: _____   Boil Time: _____

Cooling Method: _____

Original Gravity: _____ Final Gravity: _____ ABV: _____

Brewing Notes:

_____

_____

_____

_____

_____

_____

_____

Fermentation:_____

_____

_____

_____

_____

Notes on Finished Beer

Color: _____

Taste: _____

_____

_____

Other: _____

_____

_____

BEER NAME

Beer Style: _____   Date Brewed: _____

Batch Number: _____   Batch Size: _____

Specialty Grains

GRAIN TYPE	AMOUNT

Fermentables

FERMENTABLE TYPE	AMOUNT

Hops

HOP TYPE	AMOUNT	α	ADDITION TIME

Yeast Type:

_____

_____

Grain Steeping Time: _____ Boil Time: _____

Cooling Method: _____

Original Gravity: _____ Final Gravity: _____ ABV: _____

Brewing Notes:

_____

_____

_____

_____

_____

_____

_____

Fermentation:_____

_____

_____

_____

Notes on Finished Beer

Color: _____

Taste: _____

_____

_____

Other: _____

_____

_____

BEER NAME

Beer Style: _____   Date Brewed: _____

Batch Number: _____   Batch Size: _____

Specialty Grains

GRAIN TYPE	AMOUNT

Fermentables

FERMENTABLE TYPE	AMOUNT

Hops

HOP TYPE	AMOUNT	α	ADDITION TIME

Yeast Type:

Grain Steeping Time: _____   Boil Time: _____

Cooling Method: _____

Original Gravity: _____ Final Gravity: _____ ABV: _____

Brewing Notes:

_____

_____

_____

_____

_____

_____

_____

Fermentation:_____

_____

_____

_____

_____

Notes on Finished Beer

Color: _____

Taste: _____

_____

_____

Other: _____

_____

_____

_____

Beer Style: _____   Date Brewed: _____

Batch Number: _____   Batch Size: _____

Specialty Grains

GRAIN TYPE	AMOUNT

Fermentables

FERMENTABLE TYPE	AMOUNT

Hops

HOP TYPE	AMOUNT	α	ADDITION TIME

Yeast Type:

_____

_____

Grain Steeping Time: _____   Boil Time: _____

Cooling Method: _____

Original Gravity: _____ Final Gravity: _____ ABV: _____

Brewing Notes:

_____

_____

_____

_____

_____

_____

_____

Fermentation: _____

_____

_____

_____

Notes on Finished Beer

Color: _____

Taste: _____

_____

_____

Other: _____

_____

_____

_____

BEER NAME

Beer Style: _____   Date Brewed: _____

Batch Number: _____   Batch Size: _____

Specialty Grains

GRAIN TYPE	AMOUNT

Fermentables

FERMENTABLE TYPE	AMOUNT

Hops

HOP TYPE	AMOUNT	α	ADDITION TIME

Yeast Type:

_____

Grain Steeping Time: _____   Boil Time: _____

Cooling Method: _____

Original Gravity: _____ Final Gravity: _____ ABV: _____

Brewing Notes:

_____

_____

_____

_____

_____

_____

_____

Fermentation:_____

_____

_____

_____

Notes on Finished Beer

Color: _____

Taste: _____

_____

_____

Other: _____

_____

_____

_____

BEER NAME

Beer Style: _____   Date Brewed: _____

Batch Number: _____   Batch Size: _____

Specialty Grains

GRAIN TYPE	AMOUNT

Fermentables

FERMENTABLE TYPE	AMOUNT

Hops

HOP TYPE	AMOUNT	α	ADDITION TIME

Yeast Type:

Grain Steeping Time: _____   Boil Time: _____

Cooling Method: _____

Original Gravity: _____ Final Gravity: _____ ABV: _____

Brewing Notes:

_____

_____

_____

_____

_____

_____

_____

Fermentation:_____

_____

_____

_____

Notes on Finished Beer

Color: _____

Taste: _____

_____

_____

_____

Other: _____

_____

_____

_____

BEER NAME

Beer Style: _____   Date Brewed: _____

Batch Number: _____   Batch Size: _____

Specialty Grains

GRAIN TYPE	AMOUNT

Fermentables

FERMENTABLE TYPE	AMOUNT

Hops

HOP TYPE	AMOUNT	α	ADDITION TIME

Yeast Type:

_____

Grain Steeping Time: _____ Boil Time: _____

Cooling Method: _____

Original Gravity: _____ Final Gravity: _____ ABV: _____

Brewing Notes:

_____

_____

_____

_____

_____

_____

_____

Fermentation:_____

_____

_____

_____

Notes on Finished Beer

Color: _____

Taste: _____

_____

_____

Other: _____

_____

_____

_____

Beer Style: _____   Date Brewed: _____

Batch Number: _____   Batch Size: _____

Specialty Grains

GRAIN TYPE	AMOUNT

Fermentables

FERMENTABLE TYPE	AMOUNT

Hops

HOP TYPE	AMOUNT	α	ADDITION TIME

Yeast Type:

Grain Steeping Time: _____   Boil Time: _____

Cooling Method: _____

Original Gravity: _____ Final Gravity: _____ ABV: _____

Brewing Notes:

_____

_____

_____

_____

_____

_____

_____

Fermentation: _____

_____

_____

_____

_____

Notes on Finished Beer

Color: _____

Taste: _____

_____

_____

_____

Other: _____

_____

_____

_____

BEER NAME

Beer Style: _____   Date Brewed: _____

Batch Number: _____   Batch Size: _____

Specialty Grains

GRAIN TYPE	AMOUNT

Fermentables

FERMENTABLE TYPE	AMOUNT

Hops

HOP TYPE	AMOUNT	α	ADDITION TIME

Yeast Type:

Grain Steeping Time: _____   Boil Time: _____

Cooling Method: _____

Original Gravity: _____ Final Gravity: _____ ABV: _____

Brewing Notes:

_____

_____

_____

_____

_____

_____

_____

Fermentation:_____

_____

_____

_____

Notes on Finished Beer

Color: _____

Taste: _____

_____

_____

Other: _____

_____

_____

_____

BEER NAME

Beer Style: _____   Date Brewed: _____

Batch Number: _____   Batch Size: _____

Specialty Grains

GRAIN TYPE	AMOUNT

Fermentables

FERMENTABLE TYPE	AMOUNT

Hops

HOP TYPE	AMOUNT	α	ADDITION TIME

Yeast Type:

Grain Steeping Time: _____   Boil Time: _____

Cooling Method: _____

Original Gravity: _____ Final Gravity: _____ ABV: _____

Brewing Notes:

_____
_____
_____
_____
_____
_____
_____

Fermentation: _____
_____
_____
_____

Notes on Finished Beer

Color: _____

Taste: _____
_____
_____

Other: _____
_____
_____

BEER NAME

Beer Style: _____   Date Brewed: _____

Batch Number: _____   Batch Size: _____

Specialty Grains

GRAIN TYPE	AMOUNT

Fermentables

FERMENTABLE TYPE	AMOUNT

Hops

HOP TYPE	AMOUNT	α	ADDITION TIME

Yeast Type:

_____

_____

Grain Steeping Time: _____   Boil Time: _____

Cooling Method: _____

Original Gravity: _____ Final Gravity: _____ ABV: _____

Brewing Notes:

_____

_____

_____

_____

_____

_____

_____

Fermentation: _____

_____

_____

_____

_____

Notes on Finished Beer

Color: _____

Taste: _____

_____

_____

Other: _____

_____

_____

Beer Style: _____   Date Brewed: _____

Batch Number: _____   Batch Size: _____

Specialty Grains

GRAIN TYPE	AMOUNT

Fermentables

FERMENTABLE TYPE	AMOUNT

Hops

HOP TYPE	AMOUNT	α	ADDITION TIME

Yeast Type:

Grain Steeping Time: _____   Boil Time: _____

Cooling Method: _____

Original Gravity: _____ Final Gravity: _____ ABV: _____

Brewing Notes:

_____

_____

_____

_____

_____

_____

_____

Fermentation: _____

_____

_____

_____

Notes on Finished Beer

Color: _____

Taste: _____

_____

_____

Other: _____

_____

_____

_____

BEER NAME

Beer Style: _____ Date Brewed: _____

Batch Number: _____ Batch Size: _____

Specialty Grains

GRAIN TYPE	AMOUNT

Fermentables

FERMENTABLE TYPE	AMOUNT

Hops

HOP TYPE	AMOUNT	α	ADDITION TIME

Yeast Type:

_____

Grain Steeping Time: _____ Boil Time: _____

Cooling Method: _____

Original Gravity: _____ Final Gravity: _____ ABV: _____

Brewing Notes:

_____

_____

_____

_____

_____

_____

_____

Fermentation:_____

_____

_____

_____

_____

Notes on Finished Beer

Color: _____

Taste: _____

_____

_____

Other: _____

_____

_____

_____

BEER NAME

Beer Style: _____   Date Brewed: _____

Batch Number: _____   Batch Size: _____

Specialty Grains

GRAIN TYPE	AMOUNT

Fermentables

FERMENTABLE TYPE	AMOUNT

Hops

HOP TYPE	AMOUNT	α	ADDITION TIME

Yeast Type:

Grain Steeping Time: _____ Boil Time: _____

Cooling Method: _____

Original Gravity: _____ Final Gravity: _____ ABV: _____

Brewing Notes:

_____

_____

_____

_____

_____

_____

_____

Fermentation:_____

_____

_____

_____

_____

Notes on Finished Beer

Color: _____

Taste: _____

_____

_____

Other: _____

_____

_____

_____

BEER NAME

Beer Style: _____   Date Brewed: _____

Batch Number: _____   Batch Size: _____

Specialty Grains

GRAIN TYPE	AMOUNT

Fermentables

FERMENTABLE TYPE	AMOUNT

Hops

HOP TYPE	AMOUNT	α	ADDITION TIME

Yeast Type:

Grain Steeping Time: _____   Boil Time: _____

Cooling Method: _____

Original Gravity: _____ Final Gravity: _____ ABV: _____

Brewing Notes:

_____

_____

_____

_____

_____

_____

_____

Fermentation:_____

_____

_____

_____

Notes on Finished Beer

Color: _____

Taste: _____

_____

_____

Other: _____

_____

_____

_____

Beer Style: _____   Date Brewed: _____

Batch Number: _____   Batch Size: _____

Specialty Grains

GRAIN TYPE	AMOUNT

Fermentables

FERMENTABLE TYPE	AMOUNT

Hops

HOP TYPE	AMOUNT	α	ADDITION TIME

Yeast Type:

_____

_____

Grain Steeping Time: _____   Boil Time: _____

Cooling Method: _____

Original Gravity: _____ Final Gravity: _____ ABV: _____

Brewing Notes:

_____

_____

_____

_____

_____

_____

_____

Fermentation:_____

_____

_____

_____

Notes on Finished Beer

Color: _____

Taste: _____

_____

_____

Other: _____

_____

_____

BEER NAME

Beer Style: _____   Date Brewed: _____

Batch Number: _____   Batch Size: _____

Specialty Grains

GRAIN TYPE	AMOUNT

Fermentables

FERMENTABLE TYPE	AMOUNT

Hops

HOP TYPE	AMOUNT	α	ADDITION TIME

Yeast Type:

Grain Steeping Time: _____   Boil Time: _____

Cooling Method: _____

Original Gravity: _____ Final Gravity: _____ ABV: _____

Brewing Notes:

_____

_____

_____

_____

_____

_____

_____

Fermentation:_____

_____

_____

_____

_____

Notes on Finished Beer

Color: _____

Taste: _____

_____

_____

_____

Other: _____

_____

_____

_____

BEER NAME

Beer Style: _____   Date Brewed: _____

Batch Number: _____   Batch Size: _____

Specialty Grains

GRAIN TYPE	AMOUNT

Fermentables

FERMENTABLE TYPE	AMOUNT

Hops

HOP TYPE	AMOUNT	α	ADDITION TIME

Yeast Type:

Grain Steeping Time: _____ Boil Time: _____

Cooling Method: _____

Original Gravity: _____ Final Gravity: _____ ABV: _____

Brewing Notes:

_____

_____

_____

_____

_____

_____

_____

Fermentation:_____

_____

_____

_____

_____

Notes on Finished Beer

Color: _____

Taste: _____

_____

_____

Other: _____

_____

_____

BEER NAME

Beer Style: _____   Date Brewed: _____

Batch Number: _____   Batch Size: _____

Specialty Grains

GRAIN TYPE	AMOUNT

Fermentables

FERMENTABLE TYPE	AMOUNT

Hops

HOP TYPE	AMOUNT	α	ADDITION TIME

Yeast Type:

Grain Steeping Time: _____ Boil Time: _____

Cooling Method: _____

Original Gravity: _____ Final Gravity: _____ ABV: _____

Brewing Notes:

_____

_____

_____

_____

_____

_____

_____

Fermentation:_____

_____

_____

_____

Notes on Finished Beer

Color: _____

Taste: _____

_____

_____

Other: _____

_____

_____

_____

BEER NAME

Beer Style: _____   Date Brewed: _____

Batch Number: _____   Batch Size: _____

Specialty Grains

GRAIN TYPE	AMOUNT

Fermentables

FERMENTABLE TYPE	AMOUNT

Hops

HOP TYPE	AMOUNT	α	ADDITION TIME

Yeast Type:

Grain Steeping Time: _____   Boil Time: _____

Cooling Method: _____

Original Gravity: _____ Final Gravity: _____ ABV: _____

Brewing Notes:

_____

_____

_____

_____

_____

_____

_____

Fermentation:_____

_____

_____

_____

Notes on Finished Beer

Color: _____

Taste: _____

_____

_____

Other: _____

_____

_____

_____

BEER NAME
_____

Beer Style: _____   Date Brewed: _____

Batch Number: _____   Batch Size: _____

Specialty Grains

GRAIN TYPE	AMOUNT

Fermentables

FERMENTABLE TYPE	AMOUNT

Hops

HOP TYPE	AMOUNT	α	ADDITION TIME

Yeast Type:

_____

Grain Steeping Time: _____ Boil Time: _____

Cooling Method: _____

Original Gravity: _____ Final Gravity: _____ ABV: _____

Brewing Notes:

_____

_____

_____

_____

_____

_____

_____

Fermentation:_____

_____

_____

_____

Notes on Finished Beer

Color: _____

Taste: _____

_____

_____

Other: _____

_____

_____

_____

Beer Style: _____   Date Brewed: _____

Batch Number: _____   Batch Size: _____

Specialty Grains

GRAIN TYPE	AMOUNT

Fermentables

FERMENTABLE TYPE	AMOUNT

Hops

HOP TYPE	AMOUNT	α	ADDITION TIME

Yeast Type:

Grain Steeping Time: _____ Boil Time: _____

Cooling Method: _____

Original Gravity: _____ Final Gravity: _____ ABV: _____

Brewing Notes:

_____

_____

_____

_____

_____

_____

_____

Fermentation:_____

_____

_____

_____

_____

Notes on Finished Beer

Color: _____

Taste: _____

_____

_____

Other: _____

_____

_____

_____

_____
BEER NAME

Beer Style: _____   Date Brewed: _____

Batch Number: _____   Batch Size: _____

Specialty Grains

GRAIN TYPE	AMOUNT

Fermentables

FERMENTABLE TYPE	AMOUNT

Hops

HOP TYPE	AMOUNT	α	ADDITION TIME

Yeast Type:

_____

Grain Steeping Time: _____   Boil Time: _____

Cooling Method: _____

Original Gravity: _____ Final Gravity: _____ ABV: _____

Brewing Notes:

_____

_____

_____

_____

_____

_____

_____

Fermentation:_____

_____

_____

_____

Notes on Finished Beer

Color: _____

Taste: _____

_____

_____

Other: _____

_____

_____

_____

BEER NAME

Beer Style: _____ Date Brewed: _____

Batch Number: _____ Batch Size: _____

Specialty Grains

GRAIN TYPE	AMOUNT

Fermentables

FERMENTABLE TYPE	AMOUNT

Hops

HOP TYPE	AMOUNT	α	ADDITION TIME

Yeast Type:

Grain Steeping Time: _____   Boil Time: _____

Cooling Method: _____

Original Gravity: _____ Final Gravity: _____ ABV: _____

Brewing Notes:

_____

_____

_____

_____

_____

_____

Fermentation:_____

_____

_____

_____

Notes on Finished Beer

Color: _____

Taste: _____

_____

_____

Other: _____

_____

_____

BEER NAME

Beer Style: _____   Date Brewed: _____

Batch Number: _____   Batch Size: _____

Specialty Grains

GRAIN TYPE	AMOUNT

Fermentables

FERMENTABLE TYPE	AMOUNT

Hops

HOP TYPE	AMOUNT	α	ADDITION TIME

Yeast Type:

Grain Steeping Time: _____   Boil Time: _____

Cooling Method: _____

Original Gravity: _____ Final Gravity: _____ ABV: _____

Brewing Notes:

_____

_____

_____

_____

_____

_____

_____

Fermentation: _____

_____

_____

_____

Notes on Finished Beer

Color: _____

Taste: _____

_____

_____

Other: _____

_____

_____

BEER NAME

Beer Style: _____   Date Brewed: _____

Batch Number: _____   Batch Size: _____

Specialty Grains

GRAIN TYPE	AMOUNT

Fermentables

FERMENTABLE TYPE	AMOUNT

Hops

HOP TYPE	AMOUNT	α	ADDITION TIME

Yeast Type:

Grain Steeping Time: _____   Boil Time: _____

Cooling Method: _____

Original Gravity: _____ Final Gravity: _____ ABV: _____

Brewing Notes:

_____

_____

_____

_____

_____

_____

_____

Fermentation:_____

_____

_____

_____

Notes on Finished Beer

Color: _____

Taste: _____

_____

_____

Other: _____

_____

_____

BEER NAME

Beer Style: _____   Date Brewed: _____

Batch Number: _____   Batch Size: _____

Specialty Grains

GRAIN TYPE	AMOUNT

Fermentables

FERMENTABLE TYPE	AMOUNT

Hops

HOP TYPE	AMOUNT	α	ADDITION TIME

Yeast Type:

Grain Steeping Time: _____   Boil Time: _____

Cooling Method: _____

Original Gravity: _____ Final Gravity: _____ ABV: _____

Brewing Notes:

_____
_____
_____
_____
_____
_____
_____

Fermentation:_____
_____
_____
_____

Notes on Finished Beer

Color: _____

Taste: _____
_____
_____

Other: _____
_____
_____

BEER NAME

Beer Style: _____   Date Brewed: _____

Batch Number: _____   Batch Size: _____

Specialty Grains

GRAIN TYPE	AMOUNT

Fermentables

FERMENTABLE TYPE	AMOUNT

Hops

HOP TYPE	AMOUNT	α	ADDITION TIME

Yeast Type:

Grain Steeping Time: _____   Boil Time: _____

Cooling Method: _____

Original Gravity: _____ Final Gravity: _____ ABV: _____

Brewing Notes:

_____

_____

_____

_____

_____

_____

_____

Fermentation: _____

_____

_____

_____

Notes on Finished Beer

Color: _____

Taste: _____

_____

_____

Other: _____

_____

_____

_____

_____

BEER NAME

Beer Style: _____   Date Brewed: _____

Batch Number: _____   Batch Size: _____

Specialty Grains

GRAIN TYPE	AMOUNT

Fermentables

FERMENTABLE TYPE	AMOUNT

Hops

HOP TYPE	AMOUNT	α	ADDITION TIME

Yeast Type:

_____

Grain Steeping Time: _____ Boil Time: _____

Cooling Method: _____

Original Gravity: _____ Final Gravity: _____ ABV: _____

Brewing Notes:

_____

_____

_____

_____

_____

_____

_____

Fermentation:_____

_____

_____

_____

_____

Notes on Finished Beer

Color: _____

Taste: _____

_____

_____

Other: _____

_____

_____

_____

Beer Style: _____   Date Brewed: _____

Batch Number: _____   Batch Size: _____

Specialty Grains

GRAIN TYPE	AMOUNT

Fermentables

FERMENTABLE TYPE	AMOUNT

Hops

HOP TYPE	AMOUNT	α	ADDITION TIME

Yeast Type:

Grain Steeping Time: _____   Boil Time: _____

Cooling Method: _____

Original Gravity: _____ Final Gravity: _____ ABV: _____

Brewing Notes:

_____

_____

_____

_____

_____

_____

Fermentation:_____

_____

_____

_____

Notes on Finished Beer

Color: _____

Taste: _____

_____

_____

Other: _____

_____

_____

_____

BEER NAME

Beer Style: _____   Date Brewed: _____

Batch Number: _____   Batch Size: _____

Specialty Grains

GRAIN TYPE	AMOUNT

Fermentables

FERMENTABLE TYPE	AMOUNT

Hops

HOP TYPE	AMOUNT	α	ADDITION TIME

Yeast Type:

Grain Steeping Time: _____ Boil Time: _____

Cooling Method: _____

Original Gravity: _____ Final Gravity: _____ ABV: _____

Brewing Notes:

_____

_____

_____

_____

_____

_____

_____

Fermentation: _____

_____

_____

_____

Notes on Finished Beer

Color: _____

Taste: _____

_____

_____

Other: _____

_____

_____

_____

BEER NAME

Beer Style: _____   Date Brewed: _____

Batch Number: _____   Batch Size: _____

Specialty Grains

GRAIN TYPE	AMOUNT

Fermentables

FERMENTABLE TYPE	AMOUNT

Hops

HOP TYPE	AMOUNT	α	ADDITION TIME

Yeast Type:

Grain Steeping Time: _____ Boil Time: _____

Cooling Method: _____

Original Gravity: _____ Final Gravity: _____ ABV: _____

Brewing Notes:

_____

_____

_____

_____

_____

_____

Fermentation: _____

_____

_____

_____

Notes on Finished Beer

Color: _____

Taste: _____

_____

_____

Other: _____

_____

_____

BEER NAME

Beer Style: _____   Date Brewed: _____

Batch Number: _____   Batch Size: _____

Specialty Grains

GRAIN TYPE	AMOUNT

Fermentables

FERMENTABLE TYPE	AMOUNT

Hops

HOP TYPE	AMOUNT	α	ADDITION TIME

Yeast Type:

Grain Steeping Time: _____ Boil Time: _____

Cooling Method: _____

Original Gravity: _____ Final Gravity: _____ ABV: _____

Brewing Notes:

_____

_____

_____

_____

_____

_____

_____

Fermentation: _____

_____

_____

_____

Notes on Finished Beer

Color: _____

Taste: _____

_____

_____

Other: _____

_____

_____

_____

Beer Style: _____   Date Brewed: _____

Batch Number: _____   Batch Size: _____

Specialty Grains

GRAIN TYPE	AMOUNT

Fermentables

FERMENTABLE TYPE	AMOUNT

Hops

HOP TYPE	AMOUNT	α	ADDITION TIME

Yeast Type:

_____

Grain Steeping Time: _____ Boil Time: _____

Cooling Method: _____

Original Gravity: _____ Final Gravity: _____ ABV: _____

Brewing Notes:

_____

_____

_____

_____

_____

_____

_____

Fermentation: _____

_____

_____

_____

Notes on Finished Beer

Color: _____

Taste: _____

_____

_____

Other: _____

_____

_____

_____

BEER NAME

Beer Style: _____   Date Brewed: _____

Batch Number: _____   Batch Size: _____

Specialty Grains

GRAIN TYPE	AMOUNT

Fermentables

FERMENTABLE TYPE	AMOUNT

Hops

HOP TYPE	AMOUNT	α	ADDITION TIME

Yeast Type:

Grain Steeping Time: _____ Boil Time: _____

Cooling Method: _____

Original Gravity: _____ Final Gravity: _____ ABV: _____

Brewing Notes:

_____

_____

_____

_____

_____

_____

_____

Fermentation:_____

_____

_____

_____

_____

Notes on Finished Beer

Color: _____

Taste: _____

_____

_____

Other: _____

_____

_____

_____

BEER NAME

Beer Style: _____ Date Brewed: _____

Batch Number: _____ Batch Size: _____

Specialty Grains

GRAIN TYPE	AMOUNT

Fermentables

FERMENTABLE TYPE	AMOUNT

Hops

HOP TYPE	AMOUNT	α	ADDITION TIME

Yeast Type:

Grain Steeping Time: _____ Boil Time: _____

Cooling Method: _____

Original Gravity: _____ Final Gravity: _____ ABV: _____

Brewing Notes:

_____

_____

_____

_____

_____

_____

_____

Fermentation:_____

_____

_____

_____

Notes on Finished Beer

Color: _____

Taste: _____

_____

_____

Other: _____

_____

_____

_____

Beer Style: _____   Date Brewed: _____

Batch Number: _____   Batch Size: _____

Specialty Grains

GRAIN TYPE	AMOUNT

Fermentables

FERMENTABLE TYPE	AMOUNT

Hops

HOP TYPE	AMOUNT	α	ADDITION TIME

Yeast Type:

Grain Steeping Time: _____   Boil Time: _____

Cooling Method: _____

Original Gravity: _____ Final Gravity: _____ ABV: _____

Brewing Notes:

_____
_____
_____
_____
_____
_____
_____

Fermentation: _____

_____
_____
_____

Notes on Finished Beer

Color: _____

Taste: _____

_____
_____

Other: _____

_____
_____
_____

BEER NAME

Beer Style: _____   Date Brewed: _____

Batch Number: _____   Batch Size: _____

Specialty Grains

GRAIN TYPE	AMOUNT

Fermentables

FERMENTABLE TYPE	AMOUNT

Hops

HOP TYPE	AMOUNT	α	ADDITION TIME

Yeast Type:

Grain Steeping Time: _____ Boil Time: _____

Cooling Method: _____

Original Gravity: _____ Final Gravity: _____ ABV: _____

Brewing Notes:

_____

_____

_____

_____

_____

_____

_____

Fermentation:_____

_____

_____

_____

Notes on Finished Beer

Color: _____

Taste: _____

_____

_____

Other: _____

_____

_____

_____

BEER NAME

Beer Style: _____   Date Brewed: _____

Batch Number: _____   Batch Size: _____

Specialty Grains

GRAIN TYPE	AMOUNT

Fermentables

FERMENTABLE TYPE	AMOUNT

Hops

HOP TYPE	AMOUNT	α	ADDITION TIME

Yeast Type:

_____

Grain Steeping Time: _____   Boil Time: _____

Cooling Method: _____

Original Gravity: _____ Final Gravity: _____ ABV: _____

Brewing Notes:

_____

_____

_____

_____

_____

_____

_____

Fermentation: _____

_____

_____

_____

Notes on Finished Beer

Color: _____

Taste: _____

_____

_____

Other: _____

_____

_____

_____

Beer Style: _____   Date Brewed: _____

Batch Number: _____   Batch Size: _____

Specialty Grains

GRAIN TYPE	AMOUNT

Fermentables

FERMENTABLE TYPE	AMOUNT

Hops

HOP TYPE	AMOUNT	α	ADDITION TIME

Yeast Type:

Grain Steeping Time: _____   Boil Time: _____

Cooling Method: _____

Original Gravity: _____ Final Gravity: _____ ABV: _____

Brewing Notes:

_____

_____

_____

_____

_____

_____

_____

Fermentation: _____

_____

_____

_____

Notes on Finished Beer

Color: _____

Taste: _____

_____

_____

Other: _____

_____

_____

_____

BEER NAME

Beer Style: _____   Date Brewed: _____

Batch Number: _____   Batch Size: _____

Specialty Grains

GRAIN TYPE	AMOUNT

Fermentables

FERMENTABLE TYPE	AMOUNT

Hops

HOP TYPE	AMOUNT	α	ADDITION TIME

Yeast Type:

_____

_____

Grain Steeping Time: _____ Boil Time: _____

Cooling Method: _____

Original Gravity: _____ Final Gravity: _____ ABV: _____

Brewing Notes:

_____

_____

_____

_____

_____

_____

Fermentation: _____

_____

_____

_____

Notes on Finished Beer

Color: _____

Taste: _____

_____

_____

Other: _____

_____

_____

_____

BEER NAME

Beer Style: _____   Date Brewed: _____

Batch Number: _____   Batch Size: _____

Specialty Grains

GRAIN TYPE	AMOUNT

Fermentables

FERMENTABLE TYPE	AMOUNT

Hops

HOP TYPE	AMOUNT	α	ADDITION TIME

Yeast Type:

_____

Grain Steeping Time: _____   Boil Time: _____

Cooling Method: _____

Original Gravity: _____ Final Gravity: _____ ABV: _____

Brewing Notes:

_____

_____

_____

_____

_____

_____

_____

Fermentation:_____

_____

_____

_____

Notes on Finished Beer

Color: _____

Taste: _____

_____

_____

Other: _____

_____

_____

_____

BEER NAME

Beer Style: _____   Date Brewed: _____

Batch Number: _____   Batch Size: _____

Specialty Grains

GRAIN TYPE	AMOUNT

Fermentables

FERMENTABLE TYPE	AMOUNT

Hops

HOP TYPE	AMOUNT	α	ADDITION TIME

Yeast Type:

_____

Grain Steeping Time: _____ Boil Time: _____

Cooling Method: _____

Original Gravity: _____ Final Gravity: _____ ABV: _____

Brewing Notes:

_____

_____

_____

_____

_____

_____

_____

Fermentation:_____

_____

_____

_____

Notes on Finished Beer

Color: _____

Taste: _____

_____

_____

Other: _____

_____

_____

_____

BEER NAME

Beer Style: _____   Date Brewed: _____

Batch Number: _____   Batch Size: _____

Specialty Grains

GRAIN TYPE	AMOUNT

Fermentables

FERMENTABLE TYPE	AMOUNT

Hops

HOP TYPE	AMOUNT	α	ADDITION TIME

Yeast Type:

_____

Grain Steeping Time: _____   Boil Time: _____

Cooling Method: _____

Original Gravity: _____ Final Gravity: _____ ABV: _____

Brewing Notes:

_____

_____

_____

_____

_____

_____

_____

Fermentation: _____

_____

_____

_____

Notes on Finished Beer

Color: _____

Taste: _____

_____

_____

Other: _____

_____

_____

_____

BEER NAME

Beer Style: _____   Date Brewed: _____

Batch Number: _____   Batch Size: _____

Specialty Grains

GRAIN TYPE	AMOUNT

Fermentables

FERMENTABLE TYPE	AMOUNT

Hops

HOP TYPE	AMOUNT	α	ADDITION TIME

Yeast Type:

_____

Grain Steeping Time: _____   Boil Time: _____

Cooling Method: _____

Original Gravity: _____ Final Gravity: _____ ABV: _____

Brewing Notes:

_____

_____

_____

_____

_____

_____

_____

Fermentation:_____

_____

_____

_____

Notes on Finished Beer

Color: _____

Taste: _____

_____

_____

Other: _____

_____

_____

_____

Made in the USA
San Bernardino, CA
19 December 2013